U.S. PRESIDENTIAL ELECTIONS: HOW THEY WORK

INAUGURATION DAY

DANIELLE HAYNES

PowerKiDS
press.

New York

Published in 2020 by The Rosen Publishing Group, Inc.
29 East 21st Street, New York, NY 10010

First Edition

Editor: Rachel Gintner
Book Design: Tanya Dellaccio

Photo Credits: Cover Pool/Getty Images News/Getty Images; p. 4 The Washington Post/Getty Images; p. 5 Joe Raedle/Getty Images News; p. 7 (top) Rob Carr/Getty Images News; p. 7 (bottom) https://upload.wikimedia.org/wikipedia/commons/f/f3/President_Barack_Obama_with_full_cabinet_09-10-09.jpg; p. 9 https://upload.wikimedia.org/wikipedia/commons/4/4f/US_Capitol_west_side.JPG; p. 10 https://commons.wikimedia.org/wiki/File:John_F._Kennedy,_White_House_color_photo_portrait.jpg; p. 11 UniversalImagesGroup/Getty Images; p. 13 (top) Ralf-Finn Hestoft/Corbis Historical/Getty Images; p. 13 (bottom) Rick Friedman/Corbis Historical/Getty Images; p. 15 New York Times Co./Archive Photos/Getty Images; p. 16 https://upload.wikimedia.org/wikipedia/commons/5/52/TR_Inaugurationsketch.jpg; p. 17 https://upload.wikimedia.org/wikipedia/commons/e/e6/Washington%27s_Inauguration.jpgp. 19 George Silk/The LIFE Picture Collection/Getty Images; pp. 21 (top), 23 Alex Wong/Getty Images News/Getty Images; p. 21 (bottom) John Moore/Getty Images News/Getty Images; p. 25 Larry Downing/Sygma/Getty Images; p. 27 Jonathan Torgovnik/Getty Images News/Getty Images; p. 28 Bloomberg/Getty Images; p. 29 VIEW press/Corbis News/Getty Images; p. 30 Tom Williams/CQ-Roll Call Group/Getty Images.

Cataloging-in-Publication Data

Names: Haynes, Danielle.
Title: Inauguration day / Danielle Haynes.
Description: New York : PowerKids Press, 2020. | Series. U.S. presidential elections: how they work | Includes glossary and index.
Identifiers: ISBN 9781725310827 (pbk.) | ISBN 9781725310841 (library bound) | ISBN 9781725310834 (6 pack)
Subjects: LCSH: Presidents–United States–Inauguration–Juvenile literature. | Presidents–United States–Juvenile literature. | Inauguration Day–History–Juvenile literature.
Classification: LCC F196.H39 2020 | DDC 973–dc23

Manufactured in the United States of America

CPSIA Compliance Information: Batch # CWPK20. For Further Information contact Rosen Publishing, New York, New York at 1-800-237-9932.

CONTENTS

THE START OF A NEW PRESIDENCY

Roughly every four years since 1789, Americans have turned their attention to the nation's capital as the next president of the United States is sworn into office. Inauguration events, dates, and even locations have changed forms over the last hundreds of years, but the inauguration's purpose has remained the same.

Though Inauguration Day is the start of new leadership—and the end of a sometimes combative

PATH TO THE PRESIDENCY
THERE HAVE BEEN 58 SCHEDULED PUBLIC INAUGURATION CEREMONIES IN THE UNITED STATES.

election season—it's also a symbol of the **continuity** and permanence of the U.S. government.

The United States was founded on democracy, a system of government in which the people choose their leaders or representatives with elections. Every four years, Americans vote on the president, and Inauguration Day is largely a celebration of that new leader's four-year term in office.

MARK YOUR CALENDAR

Since 1937, Inauguration Day has taken place every four years on January 20. The roughly 10 weeks between Election Day and Inauguration Day are known as the transition period. This time allows the president-elect to hire White House staff and interview people for **cabinet** positions.

Before 1937, Inauguration Day was held on March 4. Lawmakers moved the date up with the **ratification** of the Twentieth Amendment to the Constitution because the vote-counting process had sped up with new technology and the March date left the departing president in power for too long after Election Day.

If January 20 falls on a Sunday, the president takes the oath of office in a small, private ceremony that day; then larger, public inaugural festivities are held on Monday.

PATH TO THE PRESIDENCY

THE SITTING PRESIDENT WHO'S WAITING TO LEAVE OFFICE AFTER ELECTION DAY IS KNOWN AS A "LAME DUCK" BECAUSE THEY DON'T HAVE AS MUCH POLITICAL POWER.

Because modern inaugurations happen at the height of winter, attendees must often bundle up against frigid temperatures and rainy or snowy conditions.

OBAMA'S CABINET 2009

LOCATION, LOCATION, LOCATION

Today, the presidential inauguration takes place outside the U.S. Capitol, which is where Congress does business. The West Front of the Capitol faces the National Mall, which is a long strip of park where hundreds of thousands of people gather to watch the historic event.

Though most inaugurations have been held at the Capitol, this hasn't always been the case. In fact, some oaths of office have been held outside Washington, D.C., altogether.

The first inauguration—of President George Washington in 1789—was at Federal Hall in New York City. Later eighteenth-century ceremonies were held at Congress Hall in Philadelphia. Each city served as the nation's capital before lawmakers settled on Washington, D.C.

Presidents Franklin D. Roosevelt, Harry S. Truman, and Gerald Ford each held their inaugurations at the White House.

PATH TO THE PRESIDENCY

IN 1929, HERBERT HOOVER'S INAUGURATION CEREMONY WAS DELAYED BY HALF AN HOUR BECAUSE FIRST LADY GRACE COOLIDGE AND SOON-TO-BE FIRST LADY LOU HENRY HOOVER GOT LOST ON THEIR WAY TO THE CAPITOL'S EAST PORTICO.

In recent years, the presidential inauguration has taken place on a platform outside the U.S. Capitol.

NOT ACCORDING TO PLAN

Some inaugurations have taken place outside the traditional time and place because of emergency situations. Perhaps the most famous case is when President Lyndon B. Johnson took the oath of office aboard *Air Force One* in Dallas, Texas, on November 22, 1963. Then-Vice President Johnson had to be quickly inaugurated at Dallas Love Field airport because President John F. Kennedy had just been **assassinated**.

JOHN F. KENNEDY

Weather derailed at least two other inaugurations, moving them indoors. In 1985, President Ronald Reagan took his second oath of office in the Capitol **rotunda** due to extremely low temperatures. A driving blizzard the night before William Howard Taft's 1909 inauguration toppled trees, dumped nearly 10 inches (25.4 cm) of snow, and forced the ceremony inside the Capitol's Senate chamber.

TAKING THE OATH

Though Inauguration Day includes many traditional events and **fanfare**, only one aspect of the day is necessary—the oath of office. Presidents may either swear the oath or affirm it. Those who choose to affirm it do so because some Christians believe the Bible prohibits swearing oaths. Franklin Pierce was the only president to give an affirmation when he was sworn in on March 4, 1853. Many presidents end the oath with the phrase, "So help me God." The wording of the oath is laid out by the Constitution. It reads:

"I (president-elect's name) do solemnly swear (or affirm) that I will faithfully execute the office of the president of the United States, and will to the best of my ability, preserve, protect and defend the Constitution of the United States."

THE VICE PRESIDENT TAKES THE OATH

JUST LIKE THE PRESIDENT, THE VICE PRESIDENT MUST TAKE AN OATH OF OFFICE. THE SECOND-IN-COMMAND DOES SO DURING THE INAUGURATION CEREMONY RIGHT BEFORE THE PRESIDENT. BEFORE 1937, THE VICE PRESIDENT HAD A SEPARATE SWEARING-IN CEREMONY FROM THE PRESIDENT. IN FACT, IN 1853, WILLIAM KING BECAME THE ONLY VICE PRESIDENT TO BE SWORN IN OUTSIDE THE COUNTRY. HE WAS IN CUBA TO RECOVER FROM A COUGH THAT KILLED HIM LESS THAN ONE MONTH LATER.

In 2009, first lady Michelle Obama held the Bible during President Barack Obama's second inauguration.

It has been tradition in recent years for the chief justice of the Supreme Court to **administer** the oath to the president. The chief justice is the highest-ranking judge on the United States' highest court. The Constitution doesn't require this practice, though. Calvin Coolidge's father, a notary public and justice of the peace, administered the oath to his son in Plymouth, Vermont, when President Warren G. Harding unexpectedly died in August 1923.

During Johnson's 1963 swearing in aboard *Air Force One*, U.S. District Judge Sarah T. Hughes became the first woman to administer the oath. In 2009, President Barack Obama had to retake the oath on January 21 after Supreme Court Chief Justice John Roberts messed up the wording on Inauguration Day!

Calvin Coolidge's father administered his son's first oath. The president took a second oath the next day in Washington, D.C., with Supreme Court Justice Adolph A. Hoehling.

PLACE YOUR HAND ON THE BIBLE

The majority of U.S. presidents recited the oath of office while raising their right hand and placing their left on a Bible—or two. The tradition—not required by the Constitution—began with President George Washington, who swore on a Bible from a **masonic** lodge.

PATH TO THE PRESIDENCY

PRESIDENT THEODORE ROOSEVELT DIDN'T USE A BIBLE DURING HIS SWEARING-IN CEREMONY BECAUSE IT WAS HELD IN A HURRY AT A FRIEND'S HOUSE IN BUFFALO, NEW YORK, AND THE FRIEND DIDN'T HAVE ONE.

President George Washington established the tradition of swearing the oath of office using a Bible before kissing the book. Not every president has done the same.

Presidents often choose Bibles with special meaning to them. Richard Nixon chose two family Bibles in 1969 and George H. W. Bush used President George Washington's inaugural Bible and a family Bible in 1989. Lyndon B. Johnson used what was at hand—slain President John F. Kennedy's Catholic **missal** on *Air Force One*.

Others have chosen not to use a Bible at all. John Quincy Adams used a law book in 1825, and Theodore Roosevelt used nothing for his unexpected 1901 inauguration after the assassination of President William McKinley.

INAUGURAL ADDRESS

After taking the oath of office, nearly every U.S. president has given an inaugural address, or speech, to lay out what they plan to do while in office. The speech sets the tone for the presidency and is usually hopeful and **unifying** after a sometimes bitter election.

The shortest speech was 135 words by President George Washington in 1793. The longest was President William Henry Harrison's in 1841, which was 8,500 words and lasted two hours! Vice presidents who unexpectedly took over for presidents who died or resigned usually gave no speeches.

Some of the most famous presidential quotes have come from the inaugural speech, including President John F. Kennedy in 1961:

"And so my fellow Americans: Ask not what your country can do for you—ask what you can do for your country."

PATH TO THE PRESIDENCY

DURING KENNEDY'S INAUGURATION, THE PODIUM CAUGHT FIRE WHILE CARDINAL RICHARD CUSHING SAID A PRAYER.

Kennedy **referenced** great speakers in history in his inaugural speech, including President Abraham Lincoln and British Prime Minister Winston Churchill.

CELEBRATE WITH SONG

As the years have passed, presidents have added their own personal touches—religious and **cultural** elements—to Inauguration Day ceremonies. Though President Franklin D. Roosevelt kept things short and simple for his fourth inauguration in 1945 due to the ongoing World War II, he added a morning worship service to the day's routine in 1933.

John F. Kennedy was the first president to include a poetry reading; poet Robert Frost read "The Gift Outright."

Other presidents have invited world-famous musicians to sing during inaugural balls and concerts before and after the official ceremony. Popular musicians Aretha Franklin, Beyoncé, and Kelly Clarkson sang at President Barack Obama's inaugurations, and Marilyn Horne and Aaron Copeland sang at President Bill Clinton's first ceremony in 1993.

PATH TO THE PRESIDENCY ★★★★★

FRANKLIN D. ROOSEVELT IS THE ONLY PERSON IN HISTORY TO BE INAUGURATED AS U.S. PRESIDENT FOUR TIMES. THE TWENTY-SECOND AMENDMENT TO THE CONSTITUTION, RATIFIED IN 1951, CHANGED THE LAW SO THAT A PRESIDENT CAN ONLY SERVE TWO FOUR-YEAR TERMS.

Beyoncé sang "The Star Spangled Banner" on January 21, 2013, at President Barack Obama's second inauguration. Kelly Clarkson sang "My Country, 'Tis of Thee" at the event.

POMP AND CIRCUMSTANCE

After the formal ceremony at the Capitol, there's a celebration as the newly sworn-in president, vice president, and their **spouses** travel from the Capitol to the White House. Since President Jimmy Carter's inauguration in 1977, presidents have walked the 1.5 miles between the two historic buildings in a procession, waving to supporters gathered along the street.

INAUGURAL TECH

IN THE EIGHTEENTH AND NINETEENTH CENTURIES, ONLY THOSE IN ATTENDANCE COULD SEE THE INAUGURAL CEREMONIES. NEW TECHNOLOGY HAS CHANGED THAT.

CALVIN COOLIDGE'S 1925 INAUGURATION WAS THE FIRST TO BE AIRED OVER THE RADIO, WHILE HARRY S. TRUMAN'S WAS THE FIRST TO BE TELEVISED IN 1949. JOHN F. KENNEDY'S WAS THE FIRST TO BE ON COLOR TV IN 1961, AND BILL CLINTON'S WAS THE FIRST TO BE STREAMED LIVE ON THE INTERNET IN 1997.

In addition to floats and balloons, marching bands, military vehicles, horses, and sometimes even elephants have participated in inaugural parades!

Procession are part of a parade of military troops, floats, and marching bands. The tradition began in 1789, when local **militias** joined George Washington on his eight-day journey from his home in Mount Vernon, Virginia, to New York for his inauguration. The parades have become more elaborate over the years.

Once at the White House, the president views the parade from the Presidential Reviewing Stand as it passes by.

DANCING THE NIGHT AWAY

The evening is when the real fun happens. The president and their spouse get all dressed up to party at as many as 14 official balls held in their honor. The balls are formal events—often referred to as white or black tie.

The Presidential Inaugural Committee hosts the official balls, which are invitation-only for donors and supporters of the new president. Other organizations hold unofficial balls throughout the capital with tickets costing up to $10,000 for a table of 10!

The new president will often try to make appearances at many of the official balls, sharing a dance with their spouse. In 2009, President Barack Obama attended 10 balls in one night! In modern years, famous singers have often performed, including Jessica Simpson at President George W. Bush's 2001 ball.

Inaugural balls are a time for the new president to cut loose and have some fun. President Bill Clinton jumped on stage with the band at one of his balls and played saxophone.

PREPARING FOR THE BIG DAY

All of these events don't just happen by chance. They're organized by the Presidential Inaugural Committee (PIC) and a congressional committee.

The PIC, which raises money for the inauguration from the president-elect's supporters, pays for much of the optional events of the day—the parade, concerts, luncheon, and balls. The government—funded by taxes Americans pay—covers the cost of things such as the swearing-in ceremony, security, and cleanup.

The swearing-in ceremony for President Barack Obama in 2009 cost $1.24 million. The entire day's events cost the government and donors about $170 million. President Donald Trump's Inauguration Day was estimated to cost up to $200 million.

Donors spent up to $1 million each for the best tickets to the day's events.

It takes millions of dollars and months of preparation to organize all the day's events.

NOT EVERYONE CELEBRATES

Though Inauguration Day events are meant to be a symbol of unity and a fresh start for the country, it often can be a day of unhappiness. After more than a year of campaigning, the losing candidate and their supporters could be angry with the new president.

Outgoing President John Adams, for instance, skipped the 1801 inauguration of his successor and vice president, Thomas Jefferson, after a difficult election. Historians disagree on whether Jefferson uninvited Adams, or Adams chose not to go.

The Women's March on January 21, 2017, called for human rights and protections for women, immigrants, and people who identify as LGBTQ.

WOMANS RIGHTS ARE HUMAN RIGHTS

PROTESTING THE PRESIDENT

OPPONENTS OF THE NEW OR RETURNING PRESIDENT HAVE BEEN KNOWN TO USE INAUGURATION DAY TO STAGE PROTESTS OF THE LEADER'S POLICIES.

ABOUT 500 PEOPLE BURNED FLAGS AND THREW ROCKS AT POLICE DURING THE 1969 INAUGURATION OF PRESIDENT RICHARD NIXON IN PROTEST OF THE VIETNAM WAR.

THE DAY AFTER PRESIDENT DONALD TRUMP'S 2017 INAUGURATION, MILLIONS OF PEOPLE MARCHED IN WOMEN'S MARCHES WORLDWIDE IN PROTEST OF WHAT THEY'VE SAID WERE HIS ANTI-WOMEN POLICIES.

In 1973, dozens of members of Congress **boycotted** President Richard Nixon's inauguration. The number of people who skipped—between 80 and 200—was hard to nail down because it wasn't an organized protest, but the Library of Congress said it was the first known boycott of its size.

AFTER INAUGURATION

For many Americans, Inauguration Day is a day to celebrate their favorite candidate's election victory. It's a great day to enjoy parties and show support for the changes to come. For others, it's a day of protest, or a day to take to the streets and march in support of a different path for the United States.

Regardless of your viewpoint, the day's historic events can inspire political interest in Americans of all ages. Perhaps consider attending the next inauguration or hosting a watch party in your hometown. If you don't agree with the policies of the new president, show your support for a new candidate in the next election or write to your representative in Congress on the issues you care about.

GLOSSARY

administer: To dispense or give.

assassinate: To kill an important person.

boycott: To choose not to attend an event as a form of protest.

cabinet: Senior political leaders chosen by the president.

continuity: A seamless or uninterrupted connection or union.

cultural: Relating to the arts or customs of people.

fanfare: A lively and colorful display.

masonic: Of, relating to, or characteristic of Freemasons (a brotherly organization with secret rituals).

militia: A military force made up civilians.

missal: A religious book used by Catholics.

portico: A structure such as a porch on a building.

ratification: Approval of a law to make it legal.

reference: To mention something said by someone else.

rotunda: A round room or building with a dome on top.

spouse: A married person or partner.

unifying: When something works as a unit or whole.

INDEX

WEBSITES

Due to the changing nature of Internet links, PowerKids Press has developed an online list of websites related to the subject of this book. This site is updated regularly. Please use this link to access the list: www.powerkidslinks.com/uspe/inaug